The Glassblowers

Also by George Sipos

Anything but the Moon (2005)

the glassblowers

GEORGE SIPOS

Edited by Sue Sinclair.
Cover photograph by George Sipos.
Author photograph by Bridget Sipos.
Design by Jaye Haworth.
Printed in Canada.
10 9 8 7 6 5 4 3 2 1

Library and Archives Canada Cataloguing in Publication

Sipos, George, 1949-
The Glassblowers / George Sipos.

Poems.
ISBN 978-0-86492-540-4

I. Title.

PS8637.I65G53 2010   C811'.6   C2009-906115-5

Goose Lane Editions acknowledges the financial support of the Canada Council
for the Arts, the Government of Canada through the Book Publishing Industry
Development Program (BPIDP), and the New Brunswick Department of Wellness,
Culture, and Sport for its publishing activities.

Goose Lane Editions
Suite 330, 500 Beaverbrook Court
Fredericton, New Brunswick
CANADA E3B 5X4
www.gooselane.com

This book is for Bridget, Emilie and Ros

The Glassblowers

ONE

Earthlight meantime

Lilacs

He loves the leaves best,
stunt spears that flop like felt,
each thrust at the chest
a feint, a half-hearted trick.

Or clouds of scent that
either rise like a fragrant cumulus,
or spill to earth in the dark space
among the leaves. Never both.
*Everything that enters the mind
enters via the heart.* Unless it's
the other way round.

Cain slew Abel for less:
for that trick with the smoke,
that phony sucking up to God
while he was busy elsewhere on the set,
missing his cue, dreaming of
making out with the ingénue among
the branches.

*Never mind the lousy casting.
Never mind the flaming sword.
The way to the heart,* he thought,
is through the chest.

Hence lilacs. Hence leaves.

Hence the garden
sacred and lost in the night.

Montford Field

It's the way heat enters through
an upstairs window
open onto fields edged with poplar,
or whether there's a breeze
or the shush of sprinklers in the middle-
distance,
              it's the heat
after all this time that enters
making glass vanish
not into transparency only, nor the desire
to lean out, nor a thirst for water as it
beads on grass, or for whitewash
and dappled shade, martins
dipping into
              and out of view

but a heat which draws the mind
out beyond the window,
beyond the plausible surprise
of summer's recurrence
to a place and time you had thought lost
but again recall
              (though you never did forget
              not one detail that mattered)

a heat you feel
radiant above the fields, waves
reflected from a canopy of leaves —
a distance that draws you
not as to an idea,

like old photographs of yourself
framed in oak,
                    but to
a world you can only enter
by chance, the way
you might suddenly discover flight

(if flying were possible)

if it were something you could tumble into,
like someone's name,
        like heat

Zodiac

Snowfall in the hills
then all the way down to the sea
till we slip into clichés:
skid, drive into ditches,
abandon everything and decide
to walk after all.

So easy to pretend
we are at the mercy of a world
outside — rain, time of day, temperature,
the small adversities that slip over us
from the windward side of the island —
meaning a trudge uphill,
meaning something we can e-mail
after supper.

But this is not the Peace River
where wind drifts snow
across roads and into mounds against
a back door frozen since at least October,
and where cattle on the neighbour's section
huddle so cold and still
you can't see them anyway
lost in so much white.

Only at the end of the dock
where the Beaver is tied till
the weather changes, and where
the Coast Guard Zodiac bumps gently
against its float, the sea black among
aluminum pontoons, and where the snow, falling,
simply vanishes,
here you might begin:

It was Wednesday. The snow started at dawn
and fell all day.

Lunar Eclipse
February 2008

What would we rather
than a gradual loss and return,
the slow solemnity
of a dun disk held above the hills?

The night at least is clear,
absence turned sacramental.

As if clarity were the point.

Ask Orion, there to the left of
the maple, the Great Nebula
sheathed at his belt like
the principal clause of something important,
its vague brightness
the syntax
of a finger raised to the lips.

We endure the interval
as does the world itself.

Earthlight meantime,
and you and I

waiting in the garden for the end.

Speechless

Driving through Quesnel past midnight
the streets are deserted, only a few lights
reflect on the river. At Two Mile Flat
the last log dumps flow by.

On the radio Bruce Cockburn talks about
his new album, the twang
of a steel guitar billowing in the car
like steam above the mills.

What does such a night mean?
Hours of driving the centreline, the road
curving left or right taking us with it,
beyond attention, automatic.

Trucks come out of the night, their lights
ablaze blinding us to disbelief.
We hold our breath as they pass,
amazed each time that we continue,
unable to say mile after mile
what alternative the dark returns.
How it feels still to be alive.

The Astronomers

That there is nothing to see
is the last thing we want to admit,
we who are here to scan the sky
after too much wine and lamplight.
We should see Atlantis tonight, someone
with a napkin said, *re-entering*
between the new moon
and something bright nearby,
maybe Venus.
               We have spilled onto the lawn
but the moon is caught in a tree and
we see nothing else,
unless that faint star in the east
in the wrong quadrant altogether,
or two white lights moving too fast
south toward the airport.

We are no wiser for this
and turn back to the house
and the arbour of wisteria above the porch.
            Behind us
deer we have not seen
stare from the edge of the forest.
Our hosts feed them each morning and we,
who do not understand, count for little in their eyes.
The deer watch us with their heedless
sober gaze, waiting for us
to re-enter the light.

Sometimes the light

Sometimes the light at dawn,
the bent trunks of arbutus glowing among fir
deceive you.

Ah, you say, *it is only red bark,*
and the yellow flesh where it has peeled,
an inner glow as of the body alone,
and turn to the tops of conifers
for the real first light.

As if the source mattered more than light.
As if there were a moment
when you could say *Now it begins.*
As if you had waited all your life
for this—the sky an abalone shell
ignited by the receding tide,
a radiance ahead of its time.

Something casual like that
the sea sloughs off.

The Glassblowers

after 1 Corinthians 13

No chance now
to remember more than incident light

glimpses through a basement window
where torches hissed gas and glass glowed
yellow and plastic, bulbed
with the breath of people who didn't matter
only the beauty they drew
from air and fire

Someone else elsewhere
painted the ornaments with mercury,
delivered them sparkling to our eyes
so we could see more clearly how
light transcends matter
and how this imperfect earth is a passage only —
whatever stars we might dream
mere pinpricks in the empyrean

No chance for us or for them
to redeem such antique innocence:
      the wonders we breathed,
       or the vapours they did
and that killed them

Too late now to put away childish things,
our blood thick with the miracles
of light, a mad residuum of flame
we can't undo

       only remember
the glass we saw cool on a basement bench,
heat and colour fading into a slow transparency,
not humming spheres but charred wood,
      dirt on the window,
       a smell of scorched sand

the dark solidity of the world seen through glass,
everything visible damned and blessed
into light

Cloud Chamber

Moths circle the lamp,
beat their heads against glass,
make the same points again and again
with the vehemence of old arguments.
In an age of open flame
they would have blazed like Jan Palach
in the streets of Prague, alight in the
brief hiss of a sanctified end.

But here they repeat
the little melodramas of bodies
flung against an indifferent current.
Turn off the light and they do not stop.
Invisible paths criss-cross the room
like neutrinos
stirring traces in the humid dark.

Why don't they settle? Find a flat surface
to cling to, make a truce with the night?
Is it fidelity to an idea,
to the afterglow of the mind's eye,
to an incandescence etched on the retina?

Or do they simply fail to notice that
the filament has grown cold,
the suns are all burned out,
the headwaters gone dry?

Whatever the cause, their stubborn
trajectories refuse to concede to the night,
till one, gone astray,
collides with my chest.
                    I feel it pause,
                    bewildered in the dark,
its unseen wings
caught between faith and doubt.

Mid-season, mid-day

If you could trust anything
you would trust this
— the stillness above fields
when the haying is done,
                    the sun white,
            three small clouds overhead
that don't matter, a few flies
whose buzz passes you by
without malice

a light breeze

Six sheep
tucked into the slatted shade
of a fence chew what they can
and trust you
because why not?
            They know spring grass will not now
swallow them, the dew of pre-dawn
no longer
ripple their wool like sand

                    Only the mid-day sun
lost on its long starboard tack

The day,
which will not end,
smells of lanolin and mock orange,
kelp

TWO

Metasequoia

Dawn Redwood
Driftwood Canyon

It's not the slope alone
that defeats us,
an unsure footing, ice
on shale, or the
tracks that would give us away
were we to cross
the wooden barrier, but

knowing we have come too late
(fifty million years, give or
take), the sun long gone
above the canyon wall where
insects are caught in stone
and where the outline of a bird's wing
lies pale and conjectural
among layers of leaves.

Does it help to know
that somewhere in southern China
(Hubei Province, 1941, to be exact)
metasequoia, previously thought
to exist in the fossil record only,
were found growing,
their delicate fronds green as ginkgo,
branches bare of snow and
thick with buzz?

What chance
we might find our way there from here?
Follow the signs backward.
Cross the creek.
Turn left.

Freighter

Sometimes at night
lights appear and disappear among the trees,
a ship sailing north
up Trincomali Channel at 3:00 a.m.

You sit by the window
(the cat lost for the night beyond the glass)
and try to remember what you once knew:
f(x) is continuous over an interval A, B
if . . .
and
a function is discontinuous when f . . .
or
        (the moon
wading in with its inevitable sophistry,
its patches of light and dark
                on the forest floor)
a function may be
piecewise continuous over a given interval
if . . .

The irrational absence, always partial,
that once stitched sunset to dawn,
who you were
to what you might yet
interpolate across the undefined space between
everything else and
                this desk,

the view of night
from this window

Memory all you know to carry you blind
across the gap:
    red for port,
    a white light glimpsed aft,
propeller turning

L&PS Railway

Run through the reasons this can lead nowhere:

rails rusted, ties rotten as far as the eye can see,
spikes so loose you can pull them out
with your fingers,
wonder about taking one home.

This was never a line for serious commerce anyway,
more a whim — Guy Lombardo
dancing away the summer at its southern end,
saxophones and seagulls, a boardwalk by the lake.
Even the end of Jumbo, struck by a locomotive
god knows when, was less fatality
than circus act
caught in old photographs of men in cravats
posing with the carcass.

So what is it you're after?
Where do you think this relic of a roadbed
can take you? Don't kid yourself
there's danger in walking the rail —
whatever engines are left endure
flower beds in parks or rust
somewhere in a museum.
No use bending your ear to steel.
There are no vibrations,
however faint, from any distance.

Still,
you glance over your shoulder,
listen despite yourself for the squeal
of flange against curve, the thin telegraphy
that runs ahead of itself through you
to whatever vanishing point you or sunlight
might think to imagine.

A squeal growing into a rumble,
ground beginning to shake.
The cameras ready.

Sooke Harbour

On a fishing boat moored
among yachts across the bay
someone is pounding on metal—
not the clang of a bell on a buoy
swaying languorously
beyond the harbour-mouth,
but a brutish *whack whack* I can
make no sense of, nor tell what might
need such bluntness to make a fit,
to disengage shaft from bushing or
a whatever from the grip of rust.

I might understand if I lived nearer the sea
but then perhaps fail to notice
the gull beside me on the dock tilt its head,
one round eye scanning the sky, the other
fixed on little waves among the pilings,
but intent also on watching me watch it
wondering what it attends to:
sky or waves, or both,
its mind a gear finely meshed between
emptiness and the reflective opacity of
its desire, nonchalant as any human hunger,
ready at any moment to unfurl its wings,
give a single beat,
and be already half-way out to sea.

Parle-moi

for Chloé Sainte-Marie

Late morning and mist hangs above the valley.
The day, like the neighbour's cows,
has nowhere to go. They crop grass. One raises
her rear leg and twists from neck
to spine to lick upward on her flank.

Love starts otherwise:
with a precise glance across a room
you relive after all these years,
an *éclat* less lightning than hammer blow,
as in the abattoir of your childhood
you have turned your back on.
A slap, you say, that set you breathing.

But it is the in-between we end up living,
the days of low cloud and no wind,
a grey light that endures till its fade into night,
the effort of walking round and round a room,
of preparing coffee, of saying *I need you*
with no idea at the beginning
what that might mean, no idea now
what else it possibly could.

The cattle live as they can.
They stand still, lift their heads, stiffen a moment
for the slight convulsion of the rumen,
then resume what they know
they must do.

Here is the cup, my love.
Lean toward me
            and I'll hold it.

Platonic

Swans in a circle near the shore
plunge their heads underwater,
torsos and splendid tails in the air
like a vase of tulips past their prime.
Someone must have fed them
something that sank
and for which they now reach.

A dozen ducks nearby
want whatever it is for themselves
but are kept away by
a man with a plastic bucket
who pelts them with stones:

Get away you buggers.

    (Meaning, you mere birds,
      meaning, you not swans.)

The sea further out is white, the sky pale.
A row of islands floats offshore,
reflected on salt water like the idea
of something knowable. Like beauty.

Below the surface crabs scurry
doubtless, among rocks.

The tide neither out nor in.

THREE

The minor key of the dominant

Somewhere in the city

a man smashes a mug against a wall
because his coffee has grown cold,
because the mug is blue and not white,
because it's a mug and not a cup,
because the cat scratches at the door
and because it is January and the windows are dark
and because he has forgotten to long for spring

he smashes it because he cannot speak
to the implements in the kitchen,
because he can't understand electricity
nor believe in heat or light, nor remember
the commonplace kindness of spoons,
he smashes the mug and watches the shards fall
and lets them lie because his body is too heavy
to hurl against anything

Sonata Form

I awake to birdsong
in the still light of dawn.

You know what's ahead,
as do I: the melody altered
in the minor key of the dominant:
Traffic heavy this hour
northbound on the Alex Fraser

repeated every day
till the ear can make no mistake:
that's a thrush,
that *World Report.*

And then developed into what it might
possibly mean, themes
intermingled, keys changed:

I left before noon but failed to find the Buddhist retreat on Mt.
Tuam. The road is difficult, and empty. The place closed anyway,
I had been told.

One of the last residents, who had meditated on the mountain for
six years, was asked what he would do on leaving. Have a good
time, he said, and get laid.

The mountainside is overrun with wild sheep. They graze among
the oaks. I watch a white ewe and a black lamb standing on a bluff.
Beyond them, rain clouds move over Cowichan Bay, while we stay
warm in spring sun.

Each day birds return
from wherever they spend the night.
As does day.

In Vancouver, a line of tail lights
arcs above the river.
Rain will give way to scattered clouds
by mid-day. The world turning from the dark,
there as here.

Trotsky

Victoria Day gone and squalls of rain
slant from intransigent clouds.
Leaves on the cottonwoods remain tentative,
refuse, despite the rightness of the time,
to run riot. They spread rumours of snow.

You dig about in the garden
but are unwilling to throw your faith
behind the idea of spring.
In the shed you shuffle packets of seeds:
parsley for its iron,
the red banners of beets,
promises of lettuce clutched in the air like
manifestos for a newer, a healthier,
a better-ordered world.

In Vienna rain pours down
the windows of a café where Trotsky
studies the positions of kings and queens.
A thousand miles from his native soil
he moves a pawn forward,
hears it click on the board
the way a hoe might sound
                hitting stone.

Your spade cuts through clay
and last year's roots.
You turn the soil till the blade shines.
Such is the cultivation of exile
with which you think to argue summer
into being, wield your simple tools
against inclemencies of the season.

Trotsky does not think of Mexico,
nor of the betrayals of time,
nor of the ice-pick sharpening
in a harvest of clouds.

He plays his pieces one by one.
He believes he is living in history.

For you there is the weather. A garden.

Pro-Life at the Ex

Signs ask if I know that abortion
can cause cervical inflammation,
fallopian-tube adhesions,
or, worse, perforation of the uterus.

A couple beyond all danger of childbearing
collects names on a petition
and guards a half-size model
of the pelvic cavity complete with wee
homunculus moulded in acrylic resin
and curled like the kernel of a pink nut
in solemn demonstration
of the sanctity of life.

Beside them, happy women
cut pieces of home-made fudge from
foot-square slabs in varying shades
of brown and dun
or sticky pink swirls:
Fudgesicle, Bubble Gum,
Cashew Ripple.

They wear transparent gloves.
Wield spatulas like surgeons.

Trap: Mouse, Wood

Which you have chosen over
Trap: Better, Improved
because you believe in the old ways
even in death:
> wood
> spring
> a metal flap
for cheese, a bent wire
that just barely holds the trap set
—no safety catch,
no escape clause, no
are you sure you want to delete
this file?— only a delicate balance
you hold in your fingers
like the final Jack or nine of spades
ready for the peak
of a life's perfect pagoda.

You wait at night for the scurry of feet
along a baseboard,
till the trap
snaps—
> and leaves a body
for the morning light, rigid
on its wooden slab, head caught
in the jaws of a crimson V:

Victor Brand,
someone has foreseen,
Unimproved.

Fussbad

Not derivatively, not
a little slosh of tea in a saucer,
but the thing itself, a ration of
heat and comfort steaming
within the circumference of necessity:
    a tin basin
    a room with a stove
    a ewer.

But what can we hope
such water will wash away:
the grim nostalgia of marching,
cold Novembers of ill-fitting boots,
factories and trains in the night,
rifle butts,
turnips frozen to pitchforks
in an empty field?

No warmth in such a world but blunt
utility — whatever three lumps
of coal and a handful of kindling
afford. A bivouac at best,
the briefest halt:
gaunt ankles stuck like stubble
in a circle of tin.

Still, we seek solace where we can—
at the edges of night among loops
of barbed wire and the smoke of chimneys
where the rout continues.
Regiments of plumbers herd us
toward the taps,
but we insist on this moment:
>   two feet on chipped enamel,
>   a handle heavy in our hand,
>   the last water on earth
>   ready to pour
scalding.

12 Gauge

One afternoon on the barrens, our dog was shot . . .
her head laced with birdshot.

Michael Winter

As if that were an authentication —

the retriever yelping in the heather,
or else stunned
with an irony you'll remind yourself of later
as you recall the fine
carelessness of how a boy
grows into a man,

something you can turn to
when you need a good story:
wind on the barrens,
first love, your helplessness
tinged with recoil,
a guiltless loss.

A kind of excuse
when you can't think of anything else to say
as you watch a woman
you once loved fold a blue J-cloth
in a white kitchen,
and leave it to dry beside
a cup
and three shining spoons.

After the Storm

Two nights of rain
and the forest is stripped of leaves.
The aftermath clings to our boots,
covers the undergrowth.
Trees stand about in the debris
of everything they cannot yet
believe they have lost,
hold their hands in the air.

What can we do
but clean up the mess,
vow this will not happen again,
build windbreaks (but of what if not trees?),
chronicle the month and date so
next year we'll know if the Fall
is early or late?

Tomorrow the wind will whistle
unopposed along a cold front,
shunt clouds past patches of sky as
black as broadcloth.
The stars will come out.
They will manoeuvre across the sky,
click their heels.

But here, now, in this lull
we rake leaves in the garden.
I work the rake, you the wheelbarrow.
When we get tired we trade.

We pile the leaves higher.

Smell smoke in the air.

CERN

furnish us then
with a knife and fork
to greet the dawn

with stamen and pistil
an outboard
an aliquot at least of happenstance

lest the light not rise
the salt stray to
our means' slow end

equip whatever
chance strand may whip may
collide in a dark wake

the antimatter of each
first day

also the last

Sarabande

dream a world new-shod,
as if rhetoric could
make it so — a fit
you search for, like Bach
ransacking a fading dance
for its native bones, for spirit —
a tamed stateliness,
a poise

or believe that rain
could cleanse the air of smoke,
of ash — the moon at midnight
red as a horse's refusal
to be broke,
hooves beating
on packed earth

the bow in your right hand
a rope
drawing it to the fire

FOUR

Willie Loves Lucy

not in movement

but in what precedes it
the way breath precedes the breath
that leads to speech
not the words we might say
                not the body unfolding
(a hand tremulous in light,
fingers arcing toward touch)
            not the dance begun
but

a stillness
like the mind of a mirror
before it thinks to reflect
            like the contour of your voice
like our hands seeking to explain:
            this is the world
            this is not the world
            this is the air

this is how our bodies move
this is light losing itself
                before

Intertidal

That it should take so little
for the tide to rise
    from one wave to the next,
fill the bay, return rocks to the inevitable
sub-surface.

Someone must know this,
have it written down,

    know to expect that what you waited
    a lifetime to reveal — the refracted
    emerald mess of the intertidal,
    its waving dissolute hearts
    clenching themselves raw and
    purple, the sweet brackishness
    of the world undistilled —
    should be merely a turning
    as of cyclists in their red and brown maillots
    leaning into the camber
    of the sea's round velodrome.

That it should be so obvious,
the resubmergence of desire into the flood
of one thing after another —
the ocean rising,
the moon with his
stopwatch nudging each wave,
kelp streaming inshore, sawdust,
    a taste of salt on skin.

Post-discursive

They are in love
others might say, and be mistaken,
simple words for such things
being overwritten now.
                    Only the long
fluorescent cabinet of the supermarket left.

How about Cambozola, you ask,
or Sage Derby?
Sheep's milk feta? No to Oka,
and what is
whey cheese anyway?

The questions that don't change.
Like rounds of *Moonstruck* coated in ash.

These are the choices —
the language of everything we want redefined.
Hard or soft
curds in the mouth
with an aftertaste, if we're lucky, of grass.

Yet we can't tear ourselves away.
We read the labels, make no move to cash out.
Look, I say,
            here's Wenslydale.
And you do.

Like snapdragons, like helium

or like none of it,
like itself:
mouths agape in astonishment

Red we say
and yellow
the language of pollen

desire volatilized
like the float planes that rise
above the harbour,
their wings awaft on what prevails

lighter than air

All of it
out of our hands

Willie Loves Lucy

or did in 1974

the tree unconcerned all these years
to think otherwise, content
with the slow blurring of love's edge
into a shallow *sans serif.*

A crow flies overhead.
Minutes later a bald eagle does the same.
Years from now we may wonder
if the beauty of the day had been
greater or less had their paths led them
elsewhere, otherwise.

Despite the crow's splayed wing,
the eagle's brilliant eye,
nothing leads to the promised land.

Nor does it not.

Shorelines stretch in the sun,
little waves among rocks speak gently
of everyday things: Subject, Verb, Object
and their opposites,
                              erosion
the last thing on their minds.

Frogs

2 a.m. and the frogs are at it
though diminished a little
like stars dulled as the night turns
through another *da capo* to repeat
whatever such melodies might mean,
or might have meant
when the creek still ran full, summer
not yet headed out back then

which after all
was only our throats distended
from desire or the loneliness of spring —
the valley filled with an easy
counterpoint we mistook for love,
as lost as they now are
still at it

that same old song that won't
let them quit

Here, by the gate

the Belgian and
those other lesser mares
stamp their feet in the dust
impatient to be done,
another year's idyll wearing thin

and I am here
and all these bloody apples on the trees

pick them, someone says
(possibly the wind)
that's what basements are for
to forget about spring

except there is no basement to this house,

except I have forgotten none of it:
how all April the last
hour of light lit the trees,
or what you said,
or how the white blossoms appeared
everywhere
                    as they do
among the leaves

Squall-line

Rain not far off, you wrote,
there is so much wind in the trees.

I know the air at such times,
how it comes with a different weight, a chill,
how it makes us put down the pen and look for a sweater,
how the ear too tosses,
uncertain till the falling begins.

If this were all you had to tell me
I wouldn't mind the loss,
but I think you meant more than that,
knew, as I know, there is more to
wind and rain than rain:
the soft hiss as it sweeps the shore,
the brief silhouettes it leaves,
how quickly it glosses rocks.

We watched this years ago,
you and I—a squall-line
crossing the bay,
fresh water entering salt, moving toward us.
It left no time to trace the erasure
of those few vanishing islands,
the sky.

No time to say whatever else,
in different weather, we might have said,

the rain suddenly on us,
blue ink smudged in the writing,
the ocean an unlined page.

Mt. McBride

had we not hiked those green mountains,
ignorant of windward and leeward,
or known the signs in the west
of weather sweeping in
from the Pacific, had we thought to look
down, or anywhere
but forward,
would it have changed anything
                    then or later —
the routes we followed, the camps,
how you came to be with me at all
there above the timberline,
our simple maps, a few cairns
across the scree,
the sun
dawning each day as if for the first time

Roosevelt elk pink on a marble ridge
all we now remember

Midden

We will say the brave things:

that the tide returns,
that it returns
to the white shell beach we never left,
hears the words we spoke
so fearlessly, our feet planted
amid crab claws and kelp,
the lovely rubble
we believed could redeem its ebb.

Or we will say the things we would say
if we really were brave:

that years of weather can't help
but change the shoreline,
alter the sea itself
and these piles of shells dug over daily
by dogs and otters,
by storms off the Pacific and by
others like us.

But despite everything we
tell each other now, I fear
we have forgotten what we said then.
Our voices lose themselves among the trees
unable to recall whether it was
an eagle we saw overhead or a gull,
or what exactly we understood so clearly
when at last we fell silent
and the waves touched our feet.

Beautiful, perhaps,
all these fragments; everything
we could possibly love
                    scattered here.

Interlinear

The frogs have exhausted themselves,
as has the creek. The heat of mid-day
spills over fields like
bleach on chintz, over grass and wild daisies and the
pale sepia rails of a fence. Swallows
still swoop their fine italic, transliterate
lost summers, all in lower case
because of the heat, not quite the flourishes
you may have expected
from their sun-burned turns.

This is how time delivers its cargo:
seed heads around your waist
as light as the tan bodies of birds
fallen from nests; fronds of dry meadow grass,
a cursive line like Persian poetry read aloud
by someone you once knew.

The landscape was different then, greener,
less resigned to bounty,
all birdsong newly overheard.

Now you think the ghazal is an implement of harvest,
a mower clacking down the valley to turn
at each extremity of grass.
Think how seeds exhaust themselves into grain,
their recurring language burdened, as you are,
each line entwined with the sound of a voice,
a tractor,
someone you have forgotten.
Something you never understood that way before.
             Like grain. Like frogs.

Sibyl

There was this waitress
and she poured coffee into my mug,
white with a green line around the rim,
though that had nothing to do with anything.
I could see light slosh on the brown surface
in the glass bowl
as she poured the coffee black into the white
void of the morning, you might say.

Or evening,
whichever it was.

Don't mistake this for the heart, hon,
she said. *This is Pyrex, see?*

And there's another pot just brewed
for when you're done.

FIVE

Coffee and steamed milk

Inga

cut the engine past the harbour
and catch the wind
mid-sentence — something
it's been trying to tell you
about east-north-east
or about the tide turning,
repeated in small waves
against the stern

not as narrative,
but like the gestures a hand makes
wanting to explain,
or the way you once knew
to flip a record — fingers
on the rim, thumb by the hole,
and then the deft pivot
to bring it round

a kind of seamanship
behind everything

the sail an ear you turn windward,
then feel the boat tip
as it leans to the lee,
    hear canvas snap,
    the stays hum

arco / pizz

he wants them to be
the way he imagines playing the cello:
life, a woman,
forests of aspen in October
spilling armfuls of leaves

wants the fingers of his left hand
to lift and fall
in perfect tune,
a spontaneous vibrato by his ear so
      there he can say
      and there again,
while the bow arm glides and nods assent
committing itself to whatever twilight
might name, humming long vowels
while waiting to empty itself
over fields —
up-bow and down-bow
neither up nor down but
crossing the body like breath
flowing in and out
between longing and winter

he wants snow geese above the trees,
wants to point his bow at the sky
and play a slow pizzicato —
left hand and right as close
to understanding flight
as they'll get:
     the way sound meets silence
     leaves and returns

how each string is plucked

how anything stays aloft

73

On s'est perdus de vue

Where do they go
those fine lovers when the film runs out,
when the flicker that fools the eye
ends: Iris Murdoch on her bicycle, the
dappled light of a lane that leads
anywhere but downhill, or Jeanne Moreau
freewheeling through the heart's
few minutes of montage,
Binoche among the frescoes
swinging in a flare's white light.

                        This may be
as much as there is, whatever
desire can salvage
from the cutting room floor — sunlight,
a Tuscan sky, hair blown over the eyes,
a face glimpsed as if in passing
by the negligent lens. Then darkness.

                    Minds scattered.
The reel of the heart
sealed in its can, while up in the booth
the apparatus cools, gets ready
for tomorrow's car chase, another new disaster.

                    I want to be
the last one left, the one with the broom
working the aisles for whatever
has been spilled, the last one
behind whose eyes the film still runs,
the one who turns off the lights,
finds a bicycle in the lane
and swings onto its saddle as if
he had seen it done a hundred times.
Rides off with it into the tender
luminous night.

        Cut, cut! I'll hear you say.
It's ended.

Yes, I know, I'll say —
but look,
        here we are in the credits.

Arbutus, South Shore

Because the trunk
is the colour of honey,
and also the branches

because the sea
on a morning like this
is ruffled with goosebumps,
and because what we desire on the cliff-top
is neither death nor life exactly
but something simpler —
       an arm or a shoulder curving
to catch the sun
       or else turning from us in three-
quarter profile — instants
we want to call beauty
but which may in fact be something else:
      tree
      water
a certain disposition of the visible

and we the ones left to delineate
whatever our longing and the world
can agree to:
      this is wood,
      this is honey,
    this the lucent body moving
within

Acknowledgements

To those who deliver milk,
or mail, or news of god knows what
before the day begins, whose bottles
clink like clean bells, whose
soft electric whine stops and starts
and pre-empts for the moment the day's
harsher sonic gloss.

To those who open shutters, crank awnings,
who set out metal chairs for the sun
to warm when it clears the crown
of the avenue's chestnuts.

To those whose work is such syntax —
the acts by which the day begins,
the acts by which all days begin: coffee
and steamed milk, china cups,
little oblongs of sugar wrapped in paper.

To those who sit at tables,
whose spoons catch
the day's first light, who light
cigarettes, who know what is to come,
unfold paper, dip a cube
into coffee, begin the work.

SIX

Amphibian

Elsewhere

The border when we get to it
is nothing at all
you are leaving
you are entering
one last fine day before winter

a combine harvester in a field
erases a swath
like something we barely
remember
        peeled away

windbreaks of aspen so empty
you look through them
as though there were nothing there
as though
geese standing on a slough were no
distant miracle but merely
an invisible edge
the line where departure
rests for a moment on ice
and gathers itself
before taking to the air
and moving on

Slipstream

At 30,000 feet I remember why
there is no moon,
either here or where we have been
or anywhere

an absence we might have predicted

but no stars either, or pinpoint
of light from somewhere forsaken
on the Chilcotin

only the faint edge of a wing
reflecting
the blue glow of little screens
thanking us for choosing WestJet,

that and the red pulse
flashing on a curve
of engine.
     What I know of you
leaking out below
like oil, like hydraulic fluid,
something vital lost
to the night
        to air.

Weather Report

There was a time I would have sat at the computer,
the garden outside dark or moonlit,
the things that preoccupy dreams interrupted
into a mindlessness beyond sleep,
searching for the words
at the centre of our common night.

But that time is past.

Everywhere January rain is melting snow,
and mist from ice jams on the river
drifts among the trees.

I could tell you that all the basements
of the North are flooded, that water
from eaves is drilling sinkholes in the snow,
each drop echoing from little wells.
I could tell you, but I don't.
I leave the computer off.

Sleep will come in the end,
and the radio turn on at six
to tell us the temperature and
what to expect from the weather.
We will wake again then to whatever
there may be for us to say
about how unseasonable the world now is

or what the day might,
even now, bring.

Backdrop

. . . sheets of tin once painted white, the rust bleeding
through, the edge chattering in the wind
                                            W.S. Merwin

You can still find them here and there,
the old photographs
in which you posed beside gladioli
or in the sun by the hood of someone's car,
or the one with a pineapple
or the dog you never liked but fed anyway
from the white bowl
with a chipped rim — poses to show
you were happy, years later
when no one remembers, not even you,
the dog's name,
            or what became of the glads.

It was all monochrome then,
sepia some of it, pictures rusted ahead of their time
or faded from lying flat in albums
among dates you
never thought to record —
life moving forward like that,
            the heart pumping,
            the blood within.

As it moves still
though harder to grasp — the wind
out there, the beating within —
the names of things
            slipping away:

Remember that fruit, the one
with the spikes, what was it for?
It came from somewhere.
We took a picture and I sent it to
my mother. I wonder
what happened to it
                    that fruit?

Years before that
you lean against a white building
in July, a brisk wind blowing your skirt
against your knees. The camera
doesn't register colour
but you remember red cotton,
the chafe of a hem on your knee.
You smile at the lens despite the wind,
            want to look happy.

        The shutter clicks.

And you were.

Fulford Harbour, November

Overcast. Cold wind on the water.
Two swans bob on the boat's wake.

Or so I might tell you,
were it true.

The wind yes, and sky,
even the swans,
but the white ferry is still miles distant
at the mouth of the inlet.

There's no word for wake's opposite,
for two miles of undisturbed space that anticipate
rather than follow, no trail of
consequence nor spreading vee
of spent cause and effect, just open water
untenanted by anything conscious —
              except these two swans
inventing motion for themselves between
one wave and the next,
neck and spine curved from crest
to trough, wings folded, torso fluid.

They move upwind, propelled like the ferry
as it approaches.

Above the bay, a cold front from the Pacific
slowly turns on its invisible pivot. The tide too
does something vital.

I tell you what I can:
Look how the swans yield and
how they move, how cold,
how invertebrate.
How, like the ferry, driven.

Segue

Days pass and fall happens —
fog and strange stars on nights of no moon,
the emptiness of things
that believe themselves still full,
apple trees in the valley like
reluctant witnesses
burdened with evidence.

What are you waiting for,
say it:
she's gone.

Summer took her
like your pickup truck and dog, and it ain't no use.
Winter's in the fields
tuning his guitar.

Remember spring?
Sure you do, how that song went,
the seeds you buried —
tomato and eggplant,
then sun and rain and leaves and the tart
bitter end of fruit.

Days pass from one chord
to the next —
birds gone,
leaves turning brittle.

Someone is guilty
of too much, or not enough:
empty nights
caught like shreds of cloth
on barbed wire.
Facts you don't know
what to do with.

Not you, not anyone.

The Belgian and Shire

down by the creek
almost persuade us
this is how time works — swifts
in the middle air
and a faint dust from horses' hooves,
tails swishing in sunlight like
the slow swing of escapements,
or like silk, or hair
shaken across the eyes when
someone says *no, not that*
and only half means it.

The flies circle and land again
with an easy nonchalance,

the entente of long days that will
vanish at first frost,
leaving only Pearl with her
round hooves and fine withers,
Bluebell with her blaze.

And us too —
dust gone with the rains,
the calendar of the fields
recalled to its purpose:
        swish stilled and a slow plod
        along the fence.

No, we will want to say, *not like that
not yet, not now*

        though we'll know it's no use,
no one will hear if we insist
we mean it.

A Mighty Wind

To wake to a sky
scoured white by last night's wind.

To be able to say that.

A road through hills covered with
debris we can only take as evidence,
bits of branches the Douglas fir
have conceded they can do without.

To say that and not apologize to anyone.

It is only air that shakes the trees,
a cold front that wakes us from dreams
we never quite manage to remember,
only their aftermath,
only the way they move through us in the dark,
a bent coriolis
of who knows what intent.

To wake to such presumed innocence,
as if the sky were a blank docket,
as if birds in the morning light
had turned up to witness:

We were asleep when it happened
but we saw what we saw:
a mighty wind from the west
scouring the sky.

Their exact words.

And then the trees,
and whatever else might yet be remembered
                    littering the ground.

Amphibian

The moon's slow trajectory behind trees
is not the moon but you
moving through the mind's parallax
of branch and cloud.

Perspective is all,
you want to believe.

In the damp bottom of fields
frogs rewind their million clocks.

You once thought wakefulness
merely amphibian, till the moon
distended its throat and
the pale luminescence of clouds
spun you backwards
toward dawn.

Sleep a mainspring wound.
Everything you might know diurnal.

Drift

Everything here seems more finite than it is,
which on an island
is finite enough if you ask me.

Tides suck up to the shore each day
like bogus acolytes, like tireless
worshippers of the timeless . . .
then leave.

Your desperate hold on reason
they take merely for so much rock,
your beginning middle and end for only
so many linear feet of shore
                    (especially the end).

What glue of the mind, what lunar
reel-to-reel could bend your days
into a loop,
            Moebius or otherwise,
                tide-driven or not?
What knot hold against the drift offshore?

                        Finitude
the old inner tube you cling to
when whatever is outer
slips from your grasp
leaves only flotsam
            (and not much of that)
here as everywhere
lost on the sea.

Lifeboat

Rope of course, and oars,
a book of knots,
a gaff.

A capstan and a harpoon.
Javex jugs for bailing.

Solo crossings in four volumes.
Maritime disasters in six.

Give us a shanty for
the old times we'll not see again:
Captain Thwart with his glass eye.
Oh aye, he'll tell you,
there was that and a whole lot more,
in those days
  white liners on the Hudson,
  whalers on the foam, or the night
  the *Prinz Eugen* made a run for it,
  how the sky lit up
  as the ships went down.

Tins of biscuits and a butt.
The smell of tarred oakum.

Hands forgotten at the davits,
yarns of rescue lost
in the lungs of drowned men.

A white hull
overturned on the swell,
its tackle spilled,
our last hope capsized.

Ah, but what a sea we had of it,
wouldn't you say now?
        A fine stiff blow.

Cranberry Road

It's over with,
          that which
so recently

it seems. A pretty road
winding through hills past outcrops,
the things we remembered   then
or beforehand:
          syncline
          anticline
          conglomerate

neuroplasticity the latest,
how we find new pathways—
nothing fixed, not even time.

The season's leaves on bedrock brown
          drift
          and fold,
their fall
the sharp curve of the eye.
Everything done
as we drive past,

          except that which

          whatever might
yet

Acknowledgements

Several of these poems have appeared, in earlier versions, in *The Malahat Review* and *The Fiddlehead*. The title of "*Like snapdragons, like helium*" is borrowed from Robyn Campbell. "The Glassblowers" was written for an exhibition mounted by the Salt Spring Professional Photographers group.

I am grateful to my editor, Sue Sinclair, for her meticulous ear and eye, and her even keener, compassionate mind.

Jean McKay and Donna Kane have, as always, been faithful literary companions, while Ross Leckie's patience and encouragement through long periods of silence have been both kind and comforting.

A number of these poems have benefited from the insights of fellow poets in writing groups in Prince George and Salt Spring Island: Al Remple, Laisha Rosnau, Betsy Trumpener, Jill Wigmore, Jane Goodall, Diana Hayes, Rowan Percy, Murray Reiss, Karen Shklanka, Chris Smart.

About the Author

George Sipos lives on Salt Spring Island, where he is Executive Director of ArtSpring, a visual and performing arts centre. His first book, *Anything but the Moon*, published in 2005 by Goose Lane Editions, was shortlisted for the Dorothy Livesay Poetry Prize.